Scenes from an Ordinary Life

GILLIAN A. FOX

Christian Design and Print

First published in 2007 by Christian Design and Print.

Copyright © Gillian A. Fox.

The right of Gillian A. Fox to be identified as the author of this work has been asserted by her in accordance with the Copyright, Designs and Patents Act 1988.

A catalogue record for this book is available from the British Library.

ISBN-13: 978-0-9557037-0-6

All rights reserved.

No part of this publication may be reproduced, stored in a retrieval system, or transmitted, in any form or by any means, electronic, mechanical, photocopying, recording or otherwise, without the prior permission of the publisher.

Cover design, typeset, printed and bound in Great Britain by:

Christian Design and Print, Nottingham
www.designandprint.biz
Tel: 0115 - 9166797

Contents

Acknowledgements	5
Creation	7
Shine Your Light	8
Easter Hope	9
A Father's Love	10
A Promise	11
I am Fragile	12
Undying Love	13
Unseen Cord	14
Gentle Jesus	16
A Thankful Heart	17
For Courage	18
Homeward Bound	19
Memories	20
Forgiveness	21
Confusion	22
Poppit (My Cat)	23
Answered Prayer	25
Senior Moments	26
This will do for my Roses	28
A Mother and her Child	30
Journey of Life	33

Creation

Thank you Father for the trees and the fields
For birds and hedgerows and buttercups
For clear blue skies and white fluffy clouds,
For bright sunny days and soft summer rain.
Thank you for valleys and mountain tops too,
For mighty oceans and babbling brooks,
Great winding rivers, and ponds for the ducks.
You raised mighty warriors, though some fragile in frame
Went forth with boldness, your word to proclaim.
You gave us a heart that you would live in
If we changed our ways and turned from our sin.
You gave us each other to care for and love.
We are all bound together in the family of God.
So thank you dear Father for all that you've done:
You've given so much, including your Son
That we'll have life everlasting, with you Lord in heaven
When our life here on earth is over and done.

Shine Your Light

In the dark hours of the night
I pray to you Lord:
Give me courage, because I am afraid,
Shine your light in the darkness
Folding me in the warm glow of your love.
Help me bear the pain I must endure,
Send your Holy Spirit to comfort me
And all others who are ill and afraid. Amen.

Undying Love

When night draws near and shadows fall
Think on our Lord, and tell him all;
Pour out your heart in passioned plea,
Go to him in humility.
Confess your sins in penitence,
Let him know that you repent
And he will grace you from above
With blessed peace, undying love.

Unseen Cord

Here comes the bus, thank you Lord,
It's too cold to stand around.
I scramble aboard and take my seat
So glad to take the weight off my feet.

With trolley full and shopping bags
I'll be happy when I get home,
A noise rings out a William Tell tune
On someone's mobile phone.

Thank goodness I don't need a phone
When I want to talk to you Lord
Wherever I am, on a bus, in a shop,
We connect by an unseen cord.

I don't want to be told "Please hold the line"
or "Press buttons One, Two or Three"
Whenever I call I'll get straight through
A direct line from you to me.

A Thankful Heart

Jesus saviour of my soul,
Gracious Lord I give my all
Every day I offer you
Prayers of faithfulness.

In my despair you comfort me
And give me still your light to see
And I shall always offer you
Prayers of thankfulness.

Jesus it's you that I adore.
I will be yours for evermore:
For you my heart is filled each day
With prayers of happiness.

For Courage

Dear Lord, give me knowledge to defeat my confusions,
Courage to face your enemies with your truth,
Wisdom to recognise all things good,
A gentle heart, and your love. Amen.

Homeward Bound

I can't see where I'm going
She cries out in despair.
Well open up your eyes, he said
Open wide, because I'm there.

To see what lies before you
Avoiding all the snares
Keep your eyes on Jesus
'Cause he's the one who cares.

He says he will never leave us
He'll be our comforter and guide
As we tread life's winding pathway
He will be there by our side.

So as along life's path we go
We'll never be alone
If we keep our eyes on Jesus
He will some day lead us home.

Memories

Each one of us has memories
The bad times, and the good.
How do we cope with all the hurt,
Live life the way we should?

We look to Jesus on the cross –
Our saviour in great pain
Looked on this sinful fallen world –
Forgave us once again.

Past hurts are now just memories
That cannot harm us any more
We live by grace, a prayer fulfilled
Our life in Christ assured.

Forgiveness

With God to guide us, forgiving is easy, forgetting is not. Past events are our memories. It is what we do with them that count. We can easily focus on the things that have hurt us, let them rule our lives, never recover from the bad things, but if we have forgiveness in our hearts, we can look back on our memories and see all the good things too. I had a few years of pain and heartache, but when I was able to forgive I felt the liberating freedom of knowing and loving God, of meeting Jesus my saviour. I will not forget those years. But I am humbled and blessed when I think of how much God loves me. His love for me is so overwhelming, my heart is filled with love. Old hurts don't hurt any more, they are memories left in their place; the pain is powerless now. Old hurts can build character, but if not dealt with properly can destroy lives. By giving them to God we can free ourselves to be the people God has called us to be. God forgives us much and by the power of the Holy Spirit in us we too can forgive much and know God's peace in our lives.

Confusion

O my God, my heart is filled with love for you –
My head is full of doubt.
My heart is filled with praise for you –
My head is full of arguments.
My heart is filled with joy –
My head is full of questions.
O my God, I am two people,
Help me become one;
Cast out my doubts,
Dismiss my arguments,
Answer my questions.
Help me become one Lord, so that I may
Wholly serve you in complete faith
I cry to you for help. Amen.

Poppit (My Cat)

He watches me intently
As I eat my evening meal
His eyes deep pools of amber
Letting me know how he feels.

"I know I've had my tea mum,
But I'd really like some more.
Some chicken would go down well:
Just put it on the floor.

I know you think I eat too much,
Well that's just how I'm made
I once was young with (ugh!) puppy fat,
I lost it when I played.

But now I'm getting older
And slowing down a bit
I need that extra nourishment
To keep me strong and fit.

So when you're sitting down to eat
Please think about me too
I need the extra titbits
Just the same as you."

So thank you Father for our pets
Big or small, no problem.
We give them love, and they love back
And our lives are richer for them.

Answered Prayer

Thank you Lord for hearing me
For answering my prayer
My life, my love to you I give
Please keep me in your care. Amen.

Senior Moments

I don't know what I've come for
I don't know why I'm here
I know I had to come upstairs
But my mind's gone blank, I fear.

So if I sit and think a while
I might just get a clue
I look around and rack my brains
And think, what shall I do?

I look in little boxes
And underneath the bed
I rummage thro' the laundry –
Take that downstairs instead.

So now I'm back downstairs again
With laundry in the washer
I'll have another little think –
What was I upstairs after?

Senior moments come and go
But mine come far too regular
I suppose I'll have to live with it
Till my time on earth is over.

And as I walk the streets of heaven
My mind will be no bother.
My joy, my thoughts, my song will be
All for my heavenly Father.

This will do for my Roses

There bubbled up in her garden
A stream; tho' not very deep
It flowed thro' her flowers to the patio
And under the fence to the street.

Barbara asked for help with this problem,
But no-one knew what to do
But nevertheless it got sorted
Where it came from and went no-one knew!

She has been known to herd cattle
Who've gone astray in the street.
She sent for the police and six came
All of them straight from their beat.

With the boys in blue at a loss what to do
Not one of them trained to herd cattle,
So Barbara said Boo! and the cows replied Moo,
Saying Boo did not the cows rattle.

They walked up her driveway and sniffed at her car,
Barbara hoped they wouldn't do damage.
Curiosity served, they walked back to the verge
But left in three different places a package.

Barbara was pleased as she got on her knees
And said "This will do for my roses,"
But the police were not sure, as they backed away
All of them holding their noses.

Then the farmer arrived quite by surprise,
The problem he quickly assessed.
The cows knew his voice so followed him home
To the safety of the one who knows best.

A Mother and her Child

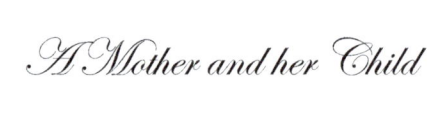

A baby's due, oh what a joy,
A baby girl or a baby boy?
Sleepness nights, endless feeds,
Having to meet a baby's needs.
Tiny fingers and tiny toes
Big blue eyes, a little snub nose,
Soft downy hair with a little curl,
Life as you knew it is now a whirl.

Now baby's toddling, what a relief,
Able to stand on their own two feet
Mind the cat's tail, watch out for the door,
Baby's toys all over the floor.
Bath times are hectic, where is the soap?
Must get a yellow duck, one that will float,
Big fluffy towels and long warm cuddles,
In bed at last, now to mop up the puddles.

And so off to school, these last years have flown,
An adventure awaits away from family and home.
Scuffed knees and torn clothing, shoes are a mess,
Your child's so excited and couldn't care less.
P.E. in the hall, finger painting in class,
Fair hair is now a bright blue and red mass,
Sports day is here, it will be loads of fun,
Three legged and sack race, just see your child run.

And then in their teens, oh what a fright,
Your sweet little child is nowhere in sight,
Into a black hole, where teenagers go!!
And out comes an alien, someone you don't know,
Answers all questions with grunts or "Whatever!"
They know all the answers, they think they're so clever,
They want to stay out late, won't clean their room
The ending of this phase can't come too soon!

Now in their twenties and working so hard
They've met someone special, letting go will be hard.
A wedding is planned either spring or the summer,
Another milestone for a child and their mother.
Two years go by and your child has good news,
They are looking at names but don't know which to choose.
A baby is due, oh what a joy,
A baby girl or a baby boy?

Father we thank you for the gift of new life,
Our children are blessings in good times and strife
They sometimes bring heartache, but give so much joy,
Whether we're blessed with a girl or a boy
We raise them to know you and hope they will stay –
In the family of God, so as parents must pray –
That our children will grow in a knowledge of you,
A heart for their Saviour they will daily renew.

Journey of Life

Help me face the New Year Lord
With you always by my side.
Each new challenge that I face
You'll be my constant guide.

I know not what lies before me
But when temptation comes my way
I'll put my trust in you Lord
Sufficient for that day.

As I go along life's pathway
With the pitfalls and the snares
I know you'll be there with me
Because you're the God who cares.

And so Lord as this year moves on
With bad times and the good
Help me Lord to live each day
The way I know I should.

And so I want to thank you Lord
For all you've done for me.
You've loved me since the dawn of time
And you died to set me free.